WATER

The Use of Water
in Landscape Architecture

WATER

The Use of Water in Landscape Architecture

Susan and Geoffrey Jellicoe

ADAM & CHARLES BLACK
LONDON

FIRST PUBLISHED IN 1971
BY A. AND C. BLACK LIMITED
4, 5 AND 6 SOHO SQUARE LONDON WIV 6AD

ISBN 0 7136 1188 X

PRINTED IN GREAT BRITAIN BY
W & J MACKAY & CO LTD

Contents

ACKNOWLEDGEMENTS

Aerofilms: p. 8 bottom, p. 30 top; Architectural Press: p. 27 bottom, p. 87 bottom; Ashford Castle Hotel: p. 118; Bibliotheque Nationale, Paris: p. 58, p. 59 top right; Brighton Public Libraries: p. 115; British Museum: p. 23 top, p. 59 top left; British Travel Association: p. 85, p. 86 (both); British Waterways: p. 28 top and centre; Calcografia Nazionale, Rome: p. 101; J. Allan Cash: p. 60 top, p. 61 bottom; Thomas Church: p. 22 (both); Country Life: pp. 88–89; Devonshire Collections, Chatsworth: p. 87 top; Rüdiger Dichtel, Stuttgart: p. 121; John Donat: p. 134, p. 135 bottom; Ente Provinziale per il Turismo, Caserta: pp. 104–5; E.P.I.T., Novara: pp. 74–75; E.P.I.T., Venice: p. 29 bottom; French Government Tourist Office, London: p. 23 bottom, p. 36 bottom, p. 77; Foto Fürstenberg: p. 38 top; Keith Gibson: pp. 131–33; M. G. Griffin: p. 17 bottom; Guildhall Library, London: pp. 112–13; Richard Huws: p. 39 top; I.B.M., Armonk: p. 39 bottom; India Office Library: p. 52 bottom; Japan Information Centre, London: p. 34 bottom, p. 62; Kroller-Muller Museum, Otterlo: p. 40 bottom; William MacQuitty (from *Abu Simbel*): p. 33; Janet March-Penney: pp. 127–29; Kenneth Martin: p. 38 bottom; Mrs. Nemon-Stuart: p. 51, p. 53 top; Michio Noguchi: p. 40; Norwich Central Library: p. 29 top; Novosti Press Agency, London: pp. 94–5; The Oregonian: p. 135 top; Colin Penn: p. 59 bottom, p. 60 bottom, p. 61 top; Pilkington Glass Age Committee: p. 137; Radio Times Hulton Picture Library: p. 8 top, p. 11 top, p. 24 (both); C. R. V. Tandy: p. 20 bottom left; Turkish Tourism Information Office, London: p. 18 top; United States Information Service: p. 18 bottom, p. 37 bottom; All other photographs are by Susan Jellicoe.

Stalactite cave near Karlovy Vary, Czechoslovakia.
The figure in the foreground (centre right) gives an idea of the scale.

River estuary, Kentra Bay, Argyllshire.

The Nature of Water

In England there is already so much water that its virtues are apt to be taken for granted. We ourselves are made of it: for as H. G. Wells puts it, "all living things, plants and animals alike, are primarily water things". Without it we could not live for more than a few days: with it we can survive, create civilisations, play with it and make works of art to express the joy of living.

This book is concerned with the poetry of water in the making of landscape and architecture and of fantasy of all kinds. Its uses have made endless artificial patterns on the surface of the earth and these in turn have enriched our lives through art and philosophy. Such a pattern may be anything from a formal little garden rill to the outline of a whole city. The examples shown here are selected from all subjects and from all parts of the world, ranging from Hadrian's Villa in the Roman Campagna below Tivoli to Sea City in the North Sea, and from the Summer Palaces in Peking to Chapultepec Park in Mexico City.

The oldest and perhaps the most spectacular natural water architecture is also that which has had scarcely any influence as an art form. This is the subterranean stalactite cavern, without light and lifeless (opposite). Man could never have emerged from this and therefore has no desire to return to it by emulating its form. Perhaps there is some affinity with the complexities of an Arab ceiling, but this may be accounted for by a different feeling: a desire to counteract and escape from the blinding immensity of the Middle East sky.

It is from scenes like the river landscape opposite that man as an amphibian emerged many millions of years ago to crawl ashore and start a habitat on land. The subconscious appeal to return to water seems to increase the more his daily life becomes remote from his beginnings. This urge towards the sea began most noticeably in Britain at the coming of the industrial age, with the creation of Brighton and other seaside resorts. Today he flies to the warmer waters of the Mediterranean.

The underlying attraction of the movement of water and sand therefore seems to be biological. If we look more deeply we can see it as the basis of an abstract idea linking ourselves with the limitless mechanics of the universe: man has always stretched out to the infinite. Note his little endeavours on land, mainly of tree-planting; the tiny indentations of the cliffs, works of nature with which he had nothing to do but with which he is closely associated; and compare these with the splendid sweep of the water on its way to the sea. We can then begin to understand why some of the curious shapes of modern art, otherwise unintelligible, should have such appeal. The subconscious within us has sensed an affinity with something that is in direct opposition to the mechanical sciences and is on a greater scale than ourselves.

The laws of nature created from water the first scientific piece of hard sculpture – the shell (opposite). Shells are not works of art as we recognise the term, but rather works of organic engineering. Their perfection is absolute. Perhaps more than any other animal shape they have moulded our sense of beauty. They are based on geometry, but biologically and not mathematically. Their shapes repeat, but not exactly. It must be admitted that while man with his hands and his instruments has created richer and more meaningful objects, he has never achieved the variety and consistent perfection of form that arise from this sculpture from the sea bed.

It was a considerable time in the evolution of *Homo sapiens* before the first works of art based on water began to appear. First, man the animal needed to provide himself with food and shelter and protection. He was driven to seek refuge in caves, but rarely in those that were damp and uncomfortable with stalagmites. The first art appeared in the primitive cave drawings and these were of land animals, with here and there a fish. The drawings were concerned with magic and, lovely though they are, it is significant that the authors of them should not have included the movement of water for its own sake. This was to come later.

Whether we are watching the ceaseless movement of the waves on the seashore or the eddies on the surface of a pool, or reflections on a calm day, the fascination of water seems almost timeless. It is romantic: romance liberates the imagination and relieves frustrations. These emotions are not peculiar to our age and it is rewarding to look back at the golden ages of history and see how men reacted in circumstances not dissimilar to our own.

In classical Rome, for instance, was there an endeavour to balance the dictator's genius for law and order with the poetic, the rational with the irrational? The age certainly expressed gentle human emotions through poets such as Horace and Virgil, whose works are redolent of the countryside. Occasionally it did so in landscape itself, although the direct impact of the

The chasm at Tivoli.
From a drawing, "Temple of Vesta, Tivoli", by W. Havell.

Giant clam *(Tridacna gigas Lamarckii).*
Shell forms have often provided the basis for the design of fountains.

works of the state upon landscape was usually one of domination. Fortunately, there still exists a landscape that seems to reflect the poetic spirit of Rome rather than that of its emperors. This is the chasm at Tivoli, crowned by the Temple of the Sybil. It is a landscape that has been created by the action of water, and above all one that has been lifted into the sublime by a single man-made but godlike object. The temple proclaims the harmony of the universe, giving meaning to the great turbulent scene above which it is poised.

It is said that a Roman emperor retired to Tivoli to cure insomnia by sleeping within sound of the falls. Today the waters immediately below the temple have been diverted to create electric power, but the rocks of the original course remain like some mighty works of sculpture (opposite). Cascades continue to crash nearby, the trees and shrubs cling hazardously to their rocks and it is still possible to recreate in imagination and in emotion the stupendous scene as it was in antiquity. In a sense the Temple of the Sybil is a stepping-stone for man on his progress from sea bed to eternity.

The Temple of the Sybil, Tivoli, today.
Before the diversion of the water the temple stood immediately above the cascade.

12

Rock forms at Tivoli.
Caused by water erosion – inspiration for the sculptor.

The cascade, Tivoli.

Water in Use

Except when running amok in floods and sea inundations, water is the most docile and powerful of visible elements that shape the land and mould our lives. Two major conditions for its use must be accepted: it must be kept in motion or it will stagnate, and with certain exceptions such as evaporation its whole movement in nature is governed by the law of gravity.

The exploitation by man of this natural power, together with the shapes and patterns to which it gave rise, can be traced from primitive times to the present day. Sometimes the shapes evolve through a cycle and return to the original. Thus the first water storage would have been made by damming a stream; this turns into a rectilinear tank, becoming monumental as on page 19; and returns to the primitive in modern times in the form of the great landscape reservoir. On the other hand the story of the fountain is a still unfinished one of continuous development. At first no more than a cleanser of insects from the surface of the water, the spray soon proved a delicious stimulus to eyes and ears. Moving from private gardens to public squares and parks and on to exhibitions, and changing from gravity to electricity as the source of power, the fountain has become one of the most potent factors in the uplift of the spirit.

The river may be said to be the original source of the art of water landscape, for at one time it was virtually the only means of transport within a civilisation. Villages, towns and cities rose along its banks. Church towers, as in the Severn valley, punctuated its length. Bridges of great intrinsic beauty linked one side to the other. Boats of all kinds lent colour and movement. In some cities, such as those of the rice countries of the east, the streets themselves were water and still are, with floating shops from which to buy one's wares.

The first artificial surface markings of any note arose in the Middle East from the transport of water itself from one point to another: straight irrigation channels above ground, circles on the surface when underground water was being tapped (page 17). Much later, the classical Roman developed the aqueduct and made it a monument (page 19): the Renaissance Roman made its terminus a splendid baroque feature (page 101).

The first canals for the transport of goods and people were those of the Chinese, whose magnificence was described by Marco Polo. In Europe the canal for spectacle but not for use reached its zenith under Le Nôtre in the gardens of Versailles, Chantilly, Vaux-le-Vicomte and others. Commercially it was still unimportant, except in the Low Countries, and it was not until the end of the eighteenth century that the canal for transport came into its own in all industrialised countries, introducing new forms to the landscape. The canals were soon superseded by the railways, but they have left, in England particularly, an image of lines of light and tranquillity that enrich the prettiest countryside and transform a slum.

Except for dramatic *tours de force* such as Suez and Panama, the making of canals almost ceased until a sudden revival a few years ago, mainly in Florida and the Bahamas. Such a revival could only take place in an affluent society, for its purpose was domestic rather than commercial. Modern machinery makes it possible economically to excavate canals out of sea swamps and create new building sites out of waste, each with its own marina. New patterns have been made by these new water towns, unlike any of the historic water towns in Europe.

The use of water for defence on land has a long history: an early example was the British lake village built on timber piles near Glastonbury. The moat as a means of defence was not, however, fully recognised until the Middle Ages. It then became the accepted practice for fortified castles to be set in water, a functional necessity which today has an aura of romance. In Holland, where much of the land lies below the level of the sea, whole cities were surrounded by moats and the control of water both for defence and for transport rose to a fine art.

Gunpowder destroyed the moated castle but the moated manor or farmhouse continued for some time, with the water as a defence against cattle thieves. It is the only form of defensive moat that has survived in the modern world for as a water barrier, as it is now called, it takes the place of a fence and enhances the landscape (page 25).

From time to time the character of water has inspired city design and given it an overriding personality. Venice we all know. The charm of its informality in conjunction with the particular formality of the buildings is irresistible and this is due almost entirely to the shape of the shoals and islands in the lagoon where the city was founded. It is not surprising that this romantic grouping of buildings combined with the light-reflecting qualities of water should have produced the greatest school of colour painters in Italy.

Very different is Holland, flat and geometrical, whose landscape gave rise to the formalism of the painter Mondrian. Page 30, an air view of Amsterdam shows the formidable geometry of a city laid out mathematically and using water both as a system of defence and of transportation.

These two cities have retained their character of water throughout history and projected it into the modern age. A singular and very beautiful third example is Yarmouth on the Norfolk coast, whose original sea character has been virtually destroyed. Today it can be detected only in a few fragments of the lanes. Yet the historic plan (page 29) was one of the most poetic water shapes ever thrown up by the tides and shifting sands.

The modern equivalent of the water city probably began with the creation of artificial islands in Miami (page 30) and continued with the marina townships elsewhere in Florida and Miami. A final project is Sea City, designed for the North Sea a few miles out from Yarmouth: a possibility for the future and one that for purely functional reasons has taken on the shape of a shell (page 137). Back, as it were, to the beginning.

IRRIGATION
(opposite top left)
Kashmir rice-fields.
The ground is terraced in shallow steps to take advantage of the slightest variation in the contours, with raised earth lips along the outer edges to contain the water in which the rice will grow. The lines of the terraces are like incoming waves on a shallow beach. A geometrical or mechanised pattern can be read instantly by the human eye and soon ceases to be of interest. The patterns of the rice-fields are based on the accidents of natural form and are non-repetitive: their appeal is unending.

(top right)
A water wheel at Fez, Morocco.
Irrigation creates its own engineering, often with great beauty of form.

(below)
Qanats in Iran: an aerial view.
The qanat is a form of underground canal invented by the Persians. Its course is marked on the surface by a line of shafts sunk in the ground at intervals of 20-30 yards to facilitate the tunnelling of the water-channel. From the air these shaft-holes look like the spoor of some prehistoric monster. They appear in the photograph as lines of white spots with black centres across the top left-hand and bottom right-hand corners. Across the centre of the photograph runs the dark line of an irrigation canal, flanked by regular agricultural patterns for part of its length. The scene is one of surface geometry.

Yerebatan Sarayi, Istanbul, Turkey.
The conservation of water has been an engineering problem in every age. In classical times, engineering was often indistinguishable from architecture, as in the huge underground cistern built for Byzantium by the Emperors Constantine and Justinian in the fourth and sixth centuries A.D.

Yellowtail Dam, Montana, U.S.A.
By contrast, the beauty of a reservoir in the modern world depends on pure engineering forms. The laws of nature are allowed to operate alone, without the introduction of art or architecture.

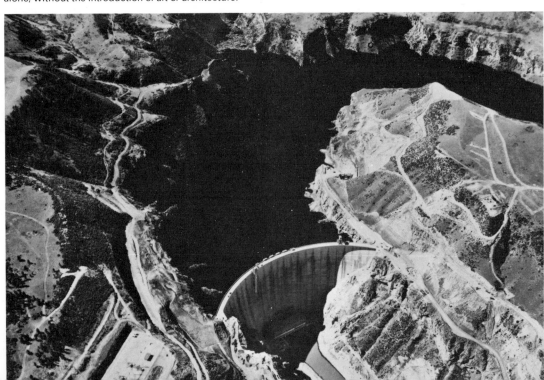

AQUEDUCTS
Segovia, Spain.
Another instance of the indissoluble blending of engineering and architecture. This Roman aqueduct is a monument in its own right.

DRINKING WATER
The Kastalian Spring, Delphi, Greece.
The Greeks regarded water for drinking as a gift from the gods. To them it had a spiritual value; the Kastalian spring, where pilgrims drank, was invested with a sacred quality.

Verbier, Switzerland.
A primitive water-trough uniting the basic architectural elements of the square and the circle.

(above left)
Cloister of San Bernardino, Urbino, Italy.
In the Middle Ages the life-giving properties of water were recognised by a well-head or fountain set in the centre of a courtyard or cloister, an idea which may have been brought back from the Middle East by Crusaders who had seen the water tanks in the centre of Muslim gardens. Over the well-head are the crossed hands which were the emblem of the Dukes of Urbino.

(above right)
Sutri, Italy.
As the Renaissance progressed the fountain became a civic feature of increasing importance.

(below left)
Rechovot, Israel.
A combined fountain and drinking fountain in the grounds of the Weissmann Institute. The wall at the back carries a quotation from the Song of Solomon: "A fountain of gardens, a well of living waters".

(below right)
Horse-trough at Salzburg, Austria.
One of the finest baroque examples, the culmination of horse-trough design.

BATHING

(left)

Woodcut of Bathsheba bathing in a garden, c. 1519.

Medieval gardens often included some provision for bathing. An amusing sequence of water from one fountain to another has been contrived.

(below)

Madresseh Madr-i-Shah, Isfahan, Iran.

A tank for religious ablutions was part of the architectural design of the main court of any mosque or madresseh (theological college). An essential feature of the design is that the water must always be up to the brim. It is therefore necessary to have an overflow channel, which is skilfully used as part of the architecture.

(right)
Plan of Sonoma pool.

(below)
Sonoma, California, U.S.A.
The shape of this private swimming pool, designed by Thomas Church, has grown from the fluidity of water forms such as the river estuary shown on page 8.

PLEASURE AND RELAXATION
(left)
A Persian garden.
An oasis in the desert, giving refreshment to body and spirit. Water was the basis of the design: narrow canals divided the garden into geometrical plots and linked the water tanks in which fountains played, as in the foreground of this 16th century manuscript. From the *Nizami Khamsah* (British Museum).

(below)
Fountains at Versailles.
There has never been enough head of water at Versailles to supply all the fountains for any length of time. Even when Louis XIV was in residence it was only possible to keep those near the palace going for part of the day. The other fountains only played on special occasions. Today, with modern lighting, they are for a brief space spectacular and stimulating.

23

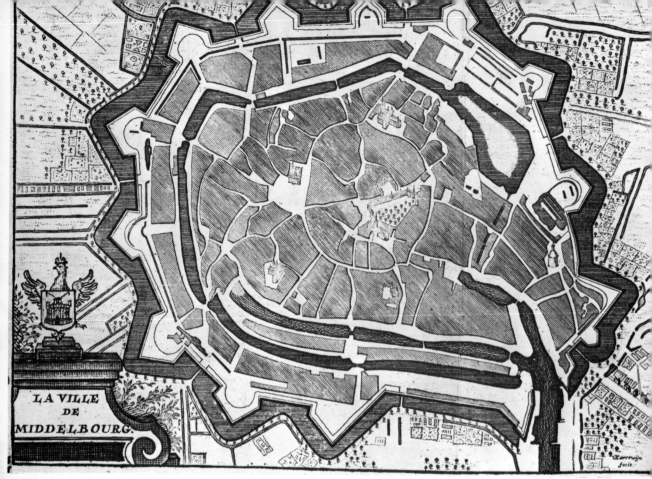

DEFENCE
Middelburg, Holland: a 17th century plan.
In Holland more than anywhere else water has been used for defence, even to the point of inundation, as in the 1939-45 war. Historic Middelburg is dominated by water: not only by the wide moat but by the access canal and internal water routes. It is a city based on a combination of water fortification and water traffic movement.

(below)
Middelburg.
The access canal is at a higher level than the surrounding ground.

Beaumaris Castle, Anglesey, built by Edward I in 1293.
A typical moated castle, once utilitarian but now romantic.

Vaux-le-Vicomte, France.
A classic example of a fortified manor, inspiring both architect and landscape architect to elaborate on the idea of water fortification and make it a source of enjoyment. The moat and the grand vista: the eye is led over the long canal that cuts across the axis at a lower level. Designed by Le Nôtre.

The London Zoo.
The water barrier is the modern equivalent of the ha-ha but makes a positive contribution to the landscape. Designed by Peter Shepheard.

BRIDGES
(above left)
Old clapper bridge at Postbridge, Dartmoor.
The space between the piers is determined by the length of the huge spanning stones.

(above right)
Cahors, France.
The medieval fortified bridge of Valentré across the river Lot.

(below)
Lake Dal, Kashmir.
A stone bridge in the 15th century bund leading from Srinagar to the Mughul gardens of Nishat and Shalamar.

Isfahan, Iran.
The Bridge of the 33 arches, which ranks among the finest in the world. This bridge and another which crosses the Zayandeh river a quarter of a mile lower down both have pedestrian footways where the people of Isfahan gather in spring to welcome the flood waters.

Wilton, Wiltshire.
A pure Palladian bridge with no serious purpose other than to look elegant in the landscape. Such features played an important part in the design of the English eighteenth century park: there are similar bridges at Stowe in Buckinghamshire and at Prior Park, Bath.

Kingsgate Bridge, Durham, designed by Ove Arup.
Historic bridges are in repose and the stone of which they are made is subject only to compression: a high percentage of the material is inert. Every fragment of Kingsgate Bridge is active, either in tension or compression, for full use is made of the tensile strength of steel as a complement to the compressive strength of concrete. The lines of the flying reinforced concrete struts have an affinity with the buttresses of the cathedral.

27

CANALS
Shropshire Union Canal in Chester.
Some of the most tranquil water scenery
we know is to be found on canals. The
canal age was in its brief prime during
the first half of the nineteenth century.
It began slowly in the 1750's and took
100 years to reach its climax, by which
time the canal was already being
challenged by the railway. The canal
introduced two new features to the
English scene — cuttings and aqueducts,
since unlike roads the canals had to be
horizontal.

**Pontcysyllte aqueduct, carrying the
Ellesmere Canal 121 feet above the
river Dee in Wales.**
It was designed by Jessop and Telford
and is over 1,000 feet long. Opened in
1805, it still carries pleasure craft to
Llangollen.

Camden Town, London. Typical urban canal scenery.
The facades of the warehouses and other functional buildings
alongside urban canals usually had a certain architectural dignity,
perhaps inspired by the water setting.

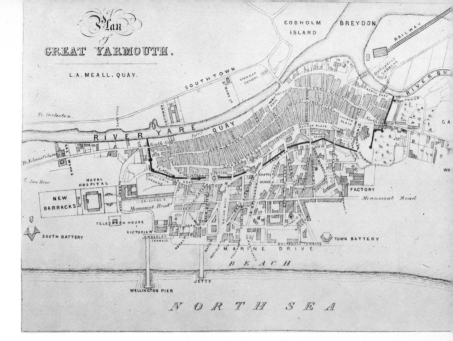

THE CREATION OF CITIES
Plan of Great Yarmouth, Norfolk.
A town whose historic shape was entirely based on water forms. The old town was built on a sandspit caused by longshore drift and has the shape of a fish, the bone structure being the lanes. Although this character has since been destroyed by modern development, it may still be detected in some of the lanes that still survive.

Aerial view of Venice.
Based on water shapes formed in the static waters of a lagoon.

Amsterdam from the air.
Built on piles on flat land, the old part of the city
has a basically geometric man-made shape.

Miami, U.S.A.
Artificial islands in the lagoon between Miami and Miami Beach (1922-26). Probably the first
modern example of the creation of sites from shallow or marshy waters. The shapes are based on that
of the individual plots of land, each with its own landing-place.

The Philosophy of Water

There is no better companion in the exploration of this subject than Izaak Walton. *The Compleat Angler* was published in 1653; in essence it might have been written at any time. Man, fish, river and landscape are dateless. Piscator is stimulated to meditation by the surface of the water: the placid river reflecting sky and scenery, always moving downstream to the sea; promiscuous eddies on the surface and ripples from a disturbance radiating in mathematical circles; rivulets cascading into the main stream. Quite suddenly, there is a bite, meditation turns to action, there is a flash from below, a struggle, and all is again quiet. Piscator's final words are:
'Study to be quiet".

Quietness and action are together the essence of all water design. Each has a philosophy of its own and the two are most beautiful when seen in combination. Nearly all the examples in this book are necessarily of water in action, but Izaak Walton is a reminder that contemplative water is the more enduring experience. One stimulates the mind, the other the eye. The one began in the Nile Valley to symbolise a future life: the other rose from the irrigation channels in Mesopotamia, ultimately coming to symbolise heaven brought to earth as an active force in the Persian paradise garden. The historic culmination of contemplative water was the artificial lake of the English School of Landscape Gardening: that of active water, the lovely carefree fountains of Versailles. Since then the idea of the contemplative lake has given way to sport of all kinds and the electric pump has opened up a spectacular future for the design of active water.

A curious by-product of the mind, but one with overriding influence, is the joint effect of symbolism and the association of ideas. The immortality of *The Compleat Angler*, for instance, depends firstly on its symbolic nature, secondly upon its image of the environment and only thirdly upon the technical information which might seem to be its purpose.

The greatest of all symbolically designed landscapes is probably that of the Taj Mahal at Agra (page 35), in which water plays a vital part. But all art is in a sense symbolic and usually the symbolism is felt rather than recognised.

One has only to enter the little flower garden in the Tivoli Gardens in Copenhagen to feel that one is in the presence of something much grander than water merely bringing nourishment to plants (page 36).

Parallel in the philosophic scale, and almost equal in its influence on our faculties of appreciation, is the association of ideas. The ancient Chinese painters taught their students to recognise in nature an analogy with the action of man: "If a great mountain is the most important part of your picture, that mountain must seem like a host and the other hills and trees like his guests". In many things, it seems, our minds unknowingly seek such an analogy and the *idea* of water, rather than the reality, can play a considerable part in the creation of ideas.

The most famous example of how the imagination can create infinity of space out of nothing is the Zen Buddhist sand garden: the quartz floor is as a sea made timeless by the ageing rocks which are set in it. In England the informal grass glades that curve through woodlands and round islands of trees are like green rivers in their sense of movement.

There are many forms of literary association of ideas, quite irrational but romantic and engaging. There are the terraces of Isola Bella which were clearly inspired by the masts and spars and horizontal lines of a ship (page 74). There is the frank evocation of the past, such as the chateau of Chenonceaux stretched across the river Cher like some tremendous medieval bridge. The Victorians were masters of the evocative and there are few more complete and nostalgic examples of escape into a Tennysonian past in time, and into a metaphysical sky in space, than the battlemented water scenery of Ashford Castle in Ireland (page 118).

The strongest pull today, however, is to be associated once more with nature. But whereas the Angler was himself a child of nature, a hunter and a nomad, we are for the most part visitors only.

The present "movement" movement in art can be traced to the age of the baroque, which coincided with scientific discoveries of all kinds. Now the world is no longer regarded as something that is constant and static: its only constancy is that of change and therefore of movement. Water is movement and there are two complementary influences that inspire all art forms arising from it: the constructivist or geometrical, which in movement is termed kinetic; and the biological, which may be termed bio-kinetic. The first emerged as a new art form at the beginning of the century, the second more recently, as an abstract idea.

Kinetic art was evolved in 1920 in a Manifesto by the sculptor Naum Gabo: "A kinetic work moves within itself, changing the space relations of the parts; and this movement is a dominant theme not an incidental quality". Gabo was fascinated by water. His brother, Antoine Pevsner, wrote: "These ideas, I believe, were invoked in him by the depth that he saw around him in the Norwegian fjords. He endeavoured to represent this depth in the things around us . . . space and time, the infinity of the universe, the entire starry cosmos that surrounds us – these were the things that constantly excited him".

From Gabo have sprung almost all the water forms of modern art: the fountain by Richard Huws at Liverpool, with its tilting buckets (page 39); the fountain by Kenneth Martin (page 38); those by Isamu Noguchi, and countless others that come under the general term "constructivist". That water can be broken into fragments and immediately re-created exactly as before is taken for granted, but it is miraculous nonetheless.

If constructivism looks to the future for its life-giving force, the arts arising from the biological sciences look to the past. Today the influence of the former is so predominant that a counter-movement seems to be taking place within us to redress the balance. An example is the swimming-pool by Thomas Church (page 22). While technological man yearns to explore the future, there is that within us which urges us to take heed of the past.

The Great Temple, Abu Simbel, Egypt (1330 B.C.).
Built for Rameses II, the seated figures overlooking the life-giving Nile are sixty-five feet high, carved from rock. There is no more stupendous example of a contemplative landscape, for the figures symbolise by their stature and sense of repose the grandeur of man and his relation to eternity. The photograph was taken before the temple was raised to bring it above the level of the new dam.

(above left)

Temple of Poseidon, Sunion, Greece (440 B.C.).

Unlike the Egyptians, the Greeks did not deify any human being. Their gods lived in the heavens, whose universal order was symbolised on earth by the temple. The close association between temple and sea acknowledges the significance of the oceans as a means of communication and exploration of an outer world.

(above right)

The Monastery of Clonmacnois, Co. Offaly, Ireland (c.900).

The great Celtic civilisation founded by St. Patrick in the fifth century A.D. survived only until the early part of the eleventh century, when it was destroyed by the Vikings. Christian monuments which still exist tell of the lovely contemplative landscape of High Cross, water and sky.

(below)

Itsukushima Shrine, Japan (dating back to 811).

The shrine is dedicated to the three daughters of Susano-no-Mikoto, a Shinto god, and is of very ancient origin. The buildings, which have been reconstructed several times, consist of the main shrine and several subsidiary shrines and buildings, all connected by broad corridors or galleries, which extend over the sea on both sides of the shrine. When the tide is full the whole edifice seems to be floating on the surface of the sea.

Ryoan-ji Sand Garden, Kyoto, Japan (1499).
The Zen Buddhist garden of contemplation reached its climax about the time that the New World was discovered. It represents the supreme use of the imagination to create an image of eternity. The sand is the sea, infinite in time and space, and the rocks are the element showing the passage of the years.

Blenheim Palace, Oxfordshire (1705).
John Vanbrugh, architect; park by Lancelot Brown, 1760. The English School of Landscape Gardening created the great contemplative lake, which appeared to be a river since both ends were concealed. The English have been masters of the creation of imaginative space.

The Taj Mahal, Agra, India (1630-52).
The view from the garden. Built by the Mughul Emperor Shah Jahan in memory of his wife, Mumtaz Mahal. The design is entirely symbolic. The building lies between the waters of the Jumna river on the one hand and the four rivers of the paradise garden on the other.

35

An artificial island on Lake Dal, Kashmir.
The island was probably made in the fifteenth century. The elegant pavilions are a later addition.

Tivoli Gardens, Copenhagen, Denmark
A modern flower garden that has something akin to the harmony and symbolism of the Persian garden — the movement of the spheres in association with the plant life of our own planet.

Chateau de Chenonceaux, Loire Valley, France (1515 - 23).
A superb poetic design to evoke the medieval romance of a building astride a bridge.

The Houses of Parliament, London (1840-60)
Charles Barry and W. N. Pugin, architects.
A romantic medieval conception based on a classical plan. This view is perhaps the best loved of any in England and the proposal to separate architecture from water by a terrace (to cover an underground road) can only be received with concern.

Falling Water, Bear Run, Pennsylvania, U.S.A. (1936)
Frank Lloyd Wright, architect. Man's defiance of the laws of gravity is emphasized by the waters below, which must follow their natural course.

37

Karlsruhe International Exhibition, Germany (1967).
Kinetic sculpture where the vertical thrust of the fountains is contrasted with the movement of waves.

Sculpture by Kenneth Martin (1961).
Fountain in stainless steel, Brixton Day College, London.

38

Tilting fountain, Liverpool.
Richard Huws (1968).
The visual and audible fascination of this kinetic design, in which sudden movement is generated by the tumbling of the water from the buckets, must not conceal that this is a fine piece of constructivist sculpture.

IBM Headquarters, Armonk, New York, U.S.A. (1964).
Fountains by Isamu Noguchi.
"The theme of this garden is science and mankind's future. A large black dome near the centre emerges from the earth to explore the universe. Diagrams of nuclear formations, stellar constellations and computer circuitry are carved in this; and critical formulas of scientific developments in the dial-like marble semi-circle at the other end. Between them is a red concavity with a fountain inside, and facing this a bronze sculpture of two inter-locking helix, the code of life." From *A Sculptor's World* by Isamu Noguchi (Thames & Hudson, 1967).

39

Expo '70, Osaka, Japan.
Fountains by Isamu Noguchi.
The tall fountain is 100 feet high: the round one of
22 feet in diameter.

Floating sculpture by Marta Pan
At the Kroller-Muller Museum, Otterlo,
Holland 1961. The figure, of polyester,
is in constant and enjoyable movement.
The sculptor designed the pool and
setting.

Memorial to airmen, Lake Trasimene, Italy.
This landscape summarises the purpose of art, whose power to create symbols can be as great in the modern world as it was in the ancient Nile Valley.

Water landscapes of the past, present and future

ITALY

Hadrian's Villa, Tivoli

118–138

The architects of imperial Rome did not share the Greek gift for placing their temples and cities so sensitively that they became one with their surroundings. On the contrary, Roman buildings seem more often than not to have been imposed upon the site with little regard for the nature of the ground.

The Emperor Hadrian's palace at the foot of the Tivoli hills, grand in scale but materialistic in spirit, sprawls across a vast area in a series of unrelated groups of buildings. Fortunately there is one unifying element – water, which perhaps speaks here for the underlying gentler side of Roman life, the world of the poets, of Horace and Virgil.

As was the custom at the time, the Emperor named the different parts of the Villa after places and buildings he had seen in his travels. The most famous of these is the Canopus. Called after a canal leading to a shrine near Alexandria in Egypt, it was once ornamented with sculpture in the Egyptian style (now in the Vatican). To make the Canopus Hadrian, like a true Roman, deepened and straightened a small valley lying between two tongues of higher ground. The canal, which is rounded at the approach end, was flanked by a colonnade which led up to the climax. This was the *triclinium*, or dining room, built in the shape of an apse, where the diners reclined on couches, refreshed by the water that cascaded down the walls and gushed through little rivulets.

The Emperor's private retreat was an island nymphaeum often called the "Marine Theatre". The design is based on three concentric circles: an outer

(above)
The Canopus, classical and serene.
It was probably intended for entertainment on a grand scale. The six statues on the right-hand side of the canal once supported the roof of a loggia. Four of them were copied from the Erechtheum in Athens.

(below)
The approach to the Canopus.
The marble colonnade combines Greek and Roman forms. The sculptures are copies of some that were found in the basin of the canal. The swans were a gift from H.M. the Queen.

The "Marine Theatre".
Originally, two wooden swing-bridges were the only means of access to the central island.

The huge basin, 177 ft by 29 ft, in the centre of the "Pecile".

circular colonnade, a canal some eleven feet wide, and a central island. On the island were a little pavilion and a garden with a fountain.

Water entertainment of a different kind was probably provided by the huge basin in the centre of the "Pecile", a rectangular space surrounded by porticoes which is thought to have been used by the Emperor's entourage for swimming games and other forms of recreation.

The Alhambra and Generalife, Granada

c. 1330–1390

The influence of the Persian paradise garden was widely diffused, but there were two main offshoots which retained intact the form of the original Persian concept. One, to the east, reached its climax in the Mughul gardens of Northern India and Kashmir. The other spread westwards along the Mediterranean seaboard, terminating in the Moorish gardens of southern Spain.

Basically the Persian *char-bagh* ("four-gardens") was a rectangular enclosed garden divided into four by water-channels representing the four rivers of life. Its origins lie far back in history, arising from the need for irrigation and refreshing green oases in a dry land but combining the mystical with the practical.

Nowhere does it live on more vividly than in the gardens of the Alhambra, itself not unlike a desert oasis in that it was built at a time when Granada was the last surviving Moorish stronghold in Spain. For two hundred and fifty years, until the Spanish conquest in 1492, the Nasrid dynasty dwelt in security behind the red walls of the fortress, gradually evolving a splendid composition of buildings and interlocking spaces leading from one to another.

Here is Moorish art at the height of its achievement and at its most characteristic, inspired by natural forms and breathing memories of an earlier way of life. Slender marble pillars recall tent-poles or, losing themselves in elaborate stucco-work overhead, resemble young trees with interlacing branches; on the ground small pools and water runnels conjure up the paradise described in the Koran: "Gardens shall they have 'neath which the rivers flow. . . . This shall be the great bliss".

Of the many courts in the Alhambra, each refreshed by water in some form, the two most magnificent are the Court of the Myrtles and the Court of the Lions. Similar in shape and size, they are quite different in character. The Court of the Myrtles, with its smooth sheet of water, was the principal court for official occasions and the court of ablutions for worshippers at the nearby private mosque, while the Court of the Lions, bubbling with fountains, formed the centre of the winter palace.

The Generalife lies above the Alhambra, across a small valley. It was the summer residence of the Moorish kings, where the ingenuity of the designers was exercised to the full in devising airy terraces, fountains and canals to bring relief from the great heat.

The Court of the Myrtles.
This takes its name from the hedges on either side of the water tank. When the Spaniards captured Granada in 1492 they fiercely repressed the Muslim religion and the practice of religious ablutions was forbidden. Tanks such as this were railed off or surrounded by hedges, as here.

(above left)
The Court of the Lions with its 124 marble columns and intricate plaster work.

(above right)
The Hall of the Abencerrages.
From a small pool a narrow water channel runs into the overflow of the fountain in the centre of the Court, underlining the interpenetration of external and internal spaces.

(below)
The Court of the Lions.
Orange trees once grew in the four plots into which the Court is divided.

(above left)
The Court of the Lions.
Twelve lions support the Moorish basin from which the central fountain jet springs.

(above right)
The Hall of the Abencerrages.
The dome is like some immense geometrical stalactite formation.

(below)
The Generalife.
The principal court with over-arching arabesque jets. The planting is gay and informal, as benefits a summer palace.

Two Mughul Gardens in Kashmir: Shalamar and Achabal

c. 1620

On the hot, dry plains of Northern India the Mughul Emperors laid out their gardens strictly on the Persian pattern, with many complaints about the dust and lack of water. To them the valley of Kashmir, where streams abound and the ground slopes gently down from the foothills, was a paradise inspiring them to greater flexibility of design and the adaptation of traditional forms to new conditions.

"Kashmir is a garden of eternal spring, or an iron fort to a palace of kings" wrote the Emperor Jahangir in 1619. Within its bastion of mountains the high wall enclosing the garden could be lowered: gazebos at the corners of the terraces look out over the surrounding rice-fields and Lake Dal. Streams were diverted to create broad canals into which fell cascades several feet high. far more thrilling than the narrow stone runnels and tiny falls, two or three inches high, which were all that could be contrived when the water had to be raised from a well, as in India.

To match the challenge of the surrounding mountain landscape and bring the gardens into scale with it, avenues of majestic *chenars* (Oriental planes) were planted, in whose shade the Emperor and his Court passed their days. For gardens were to the Mughuls much more than a place for flowers: they were a way of life. Silken tents were pitched on the grass beneath the trees and on raised stone platforms beside the cascades or overlooking the fruit blossom; stone thrones were set in the middle of the water above the chutes, called *chadars*, which are such a feature of Mughul gardens.

Here, water is not merely linked with the architecture: it becomes part of it. Rippling over the scalloped or herringbone patterns of the *chadars* its sparkle takes on their forms: the straight cascades assumed a third dimension when behind them, in tiny recesses, were set gold vases of flowers by day and lights by night.

Royal gardens such as Shalamar and Achabal were divided into three terraces: the public garden, where the Emperor sat in audience each day, the Emperor's private garden and, at the top, the zenana garden for the harem. Shalamar is a sequence of three square gardens threaded on a broad central water-course that continues beyond the garden as a canal link with Lake Dal, making one grand landscape complex. The garden was begun by the Emperor Jahangir and completed by his son, Shah Jahan, who built the black marble pavilion that is the main architectural feature.

Achabal, rather earlier in date and some distance south of Lake Dal, is thought to have been laid out by Nur Jahan, Jahangir's beautiful and talented Empress. It is watered by a spring which gushes out from the hillside with such force that there is enough water for two side canals as well as the central cascade and pools.

These gardens are the mature achievement of a dynasty founded at the beginning of the 16th century, for whom the making of gardens was an abiding passion. Each succeeding Emperor, from Babur onwards, devoted endless energy, time and money to perfecting an art which reached its culmination in Shah Jahan's Taj Mahal.

Shalamar.
Shah Jahan's black marble pavilion in the zenana garden. In Mughul times the water would have sprung up in a single low plume and not as a spray.

(right)
Shalamar.
A double cascade leads water from the topmost terrace into the basin surrounding the black pavilion. The recesses for lights can be seen below the projecting ledge over which the water falls in one straight sheet. From the pavilion there are fine views of the encircling mountains.

(below)
Shalamar.
From the black pavilion the central water-course, called the Shah Nahr, runs down to Lake Dal. On either side of the chenar trees are the traditional orchards.

(above)
Shalamar.
The stone water throne in front of the cascade that falls between the foundations of what was once the Hall of Private Audience in the Emperor's garden. A smaller stone throne is set in the middle of the cascade. Most Mughul gardens were approached from the lowest terrace, giving a sense of mystery and anticipation to the upper terraces.

(below)
Achabal: the lowest terrace.
Some of the fountains still send up plumes of water as in Mughul days.

Achabal from the top terrace.
The pavilions are Kashmiri, built on the old Mughul bases.

Achabal.
One of the side chadars with patterned surface to break up the water. It is tilted to catch the light.

Achabal
The big cascade, with stepping stones across the top, seen from the island pavilion. In other Mughul gardens the water is almost noiseless but here the air is filled with rushing sound.

55

CHINA

Imperial Peking

The Old Summer Palace (Yüan Ming Yüan – The Perfect and Brilliant Garden)

The New Summer Palace (Wan Shou Shan – The Mountain of Innumerable Years)

The centuries-old traditions of the Chinese garden had their roots in a deep-felt desire for harmony with untamed nature. Direct imitation of nature was not, however, the aim of the great painters who were largely responsible for creating the traditional gardens, but rather the weaving together of the elements of nature in an art form which would stir the imagination.

Trees and flowers, meandering paths and enclosing walls played their part, but the essential ingredients were mountains and water. The Taoist philosophy held that rivers were the arteries of the earth: water was therefore in a double sense the life-giving force. It was also the medium for creating atmosphere, catching the light or revealing mysterious caverns in its shadowy reflections. "The mirror of the pond reflects the shadows; here is opened an entrance to the mermaid's palace" wrote the author of *Yüan Yeh*, a Chinese gardening treatise. "Mountains" were made from the soil dug out to make lakes, or were suggested by rocks, and here again water played a part, for the most-sought-after were river rocks which had been hollowed out by the force of the stream.

The ideal Chinese garden was never to be seen as a whole but unfolded itself gradually in strolling along the paths which "meandered like playing cats", leading perhaps from one pavilion to another. The pavilions themselves were geometrical in shape, complementing the organic shapes of the mountains, pools and paths. They often had special uses, such as for viewing the moon, the snow on the mountains or the plum blossom. They were for the most part open structures where inside and outside were almost indistinguishable and contact with nature unimpeded. "Roll up the bamboo blind and let the swallows fly in with the wind". *(Yüan Yeh.)*

The Old Summer Palace, which was the work of two great Manchu Emperors, K'ang Hsi (1662–1722) and Ch'ien Lung (1735–96), was designed in accordance with these long-standing traditions. It was completely destroyed in the nineteenth century but lives on in paintings and woodcuts and in contemporary accounts such as that of Father Attiret, a French missionary employed as a painter by the Emperor Ch'ien Lung in 1752:

"As for the Pleasure-houses, they are really charming. They stand in a vast Compass of Ground. They have raised Hills, from 20 to 60 Foot high; which form a great Number of little Valleys between them. The Bottoms of these Valleys are water'd with clear Streams; which run on till they join together, and form large Pieces of Water and Lakes . . .

They go from one of the Valleys to another, not by formal strait Walks as in Europe; but by various Turnings and Windings, adorn'd on the Sides with little Pavilions and charming Grottos: and each of these Valleys is diversify'd from all the rest, both by their manner of laying out the Ground, and in the Structure and Disposition of its Buildings.

All the Risings and Hills are sprinkled with Trees; and particularly with Flowering-trees, which are here very common. The sides of the Canals, or lesser streams, are not faced (as they are with us) with smooth Stone, and in a strait Line: but look rude and rustic, with different Pieces of Rock, some of which jut out, and others recede inwards; and are placed with so much Art that you would take it to be the Work of Nature. . . . The Banks are sprinkled with Flowers: which rise up even thro' the Hollows in the Rock-work, as if they had been produced there naturally . . .

On your entrance into each Valley, you see its Buildings before you. All the Front is a Colonnade with Windows between the Pillars. The Wood-work is gilded, painted, and varnish'd. The Roofs too are cover'd with varnish'd Tiles of different Colours; Red, Yellow, Blue, Green and Purple: which by their proper Mixtures and their manner of placeing them, form an agreeable Variety of Compartments and Designs. Almost all these Buildings are only one Story high; and their Floors are raised from Two to Eight Foot above the Ground. You go up to them, not by regular Stone Steps, but by a rough sort of Rock-work; form'd as if here had been so many Steps produced there by Nature . . .

To let you see the Beauty of this charming Spot in its greatest Perfection, I should wish to have you transported hither when the Lake is all cover'd with Boats; either gilt, or varnish'd: as it is sometimes for taking the Air; sometimes for fishing; and sometimes for Justs and Combats, and other Diversions, upon the Water: but above all, on some fine Night, when the

Fireworks are play'd off there; at which time they have Illuminations in all the Palaces, all the Boats and almost every Tree . . .

There is this Symmetry, this beautiful Order and Disposition, too in China; and particularly, in the Emperor's Palace at Pekin . . . But in their Pleasure-houses they rather chuse a beautiful Disorder and a wandering, as far as possible from all the Rules of Art. They go entirely on this Principle, 'That what they are to represent there, is a natural and wild View of the Country; a rural Retirement, and not a Palace form'd according to all the Rules of Art.' '' ★

The first New Summer Palace was built at much the same time as the Old Summer Palace and was also destroyed in 1860 but was rebuilt on the old lines some twenty years later. It has survived, relatively intact, to give some idea of the scale of the Imperial pleasure grounds and the delicacy and beauty of their details.

★ From *A particular account of the Emperor of China's Gardens near Pekin*: in a letter from F. Attiret . . . Translated from the French by Sir Harry Beaumont. Printed for R. Dodsley, 1752.

Old Summer Palace.
Wind and Lotus, the tavern of fermented wine. In the background is a small village with shops, built to give the Emperor an opportunity to experience the sensations of workaday life and commerce, from which he was cut off when isolated in his palace. *Painting by T'ang Tai and Shen Yuan.*

Old Summer Palace.

(left)
The palace of Fang Hu Sheng Ching, built on marble terraces rising from the water. The roof was of gilded tiles, the pillars and beams deep red. *Engraving by Lerouge from a Chinese woodcut.*

(right)
A romantic enclave on the shores of the largest lake, Fu Hai (Lake of Happiness), which was said to be five miles round. *Painting by T'ang Tai and Shen Yuan.*

(below)
New Summer Palace.
K'un Ming Hu, an artificial lake, and the Bridge of the Seventeen Arches. Sham sea-battles were staged here.

New Summer Palace.
The Bridge of the Seventeen Arches leading to the island with the sanctuary of the Dragon King.

(below)
The Camel Bridge, with the Jade Fountain in the distance.

New Summer Palace.
(left)
The lake frozen in winter.

(below)
The marble boat.

Two Japanese Gardens in Kyoto

Katsura Imperial Villa

Garden of the Sento Gosho

c. 1620–1663

The great Chinese painters and philosophers were largely responsible for establishing their country's traditions of garden design. In Japan it was for the most part the Buddhist monks who, in the sixteenth and seventeenth centuries, created a series of gardens which have served as models for Japanese designers ever since. The influence of Chinese art which had spread to Japan at the same time as Buddhism in the sixth and seventh centuries had by that time waned and a native style evolved, in painting, architecture, garden design and flower arrangement. In all these arts Zen Buddhism played an important part.

Kyoto, the capital of Japan from 794 to 1868, was the centre of much of this activity and saw the creation, in the sixteenth and seventeenth centuries, of many superb gardens, some of which still survive. The character of these gardens varied: gardens of contemplation such as Ryoan-ji and Daisen-in, gardens of the "borrowed" landscape, tea gardens and gardens of movement or stroll gardens, of which Katsura is the classic example.

Built as a summer residence for an Imperial Prince, the Villa was originally reached by boat from Kyoto, down the Katsura river. Today this prolongation of the delights of water can no longer be enjoyed and Katsura is a tree-enclosed waterscape of pavilions, lakes and islands, in which the architecture plays a subordinate role.

Within this enclosed space is an intimate landscape which is a sublimation of the landscape outside, with mountains, sea and islands. It is not, however, naturalistic, but expresses the concept that man is one with nature. Every stone has been carefully chosen for its power to convey some truth about nature. Every leaf seems significant. With perceptions thus heightened the visitor moves round the garden from one unfolding scene to the next and always the water carries his imagination out of the picture as it vanishes behind interlocking land-forms.

The Sento Gosho was a palace built in 1571 as a residence for retired emperors, but it no longer exists. The garden was made at about the same time as Katsura and was designed by Kobori Enshu who is also thought to have been partly responsible for Katsura. The garden is divided into two parts, each with a small lake. The north part is on similar lines to Katsura but the south part is more open in character, its main feature being a long beach of water-washed stones.

Katsura from the air.
Here and there the path that threads round the garden can be seen emerging from the trees.

(above)
Katsura: the tea-house.
At the tip of the stony peninsula in the foreground stands a traditional stone lantern.

(below left)
Katsura.
The water disappears into infinity, its course concealed by the islands. Weathered stones such as those on the lake shore played an important part in the composition and were chosen and sited with meticulous care.

(below right)
Sento Gosho: the south lake.
The beach, each pebble of which was selected individually, slopes down to the lake from the site of the old palace.

**Sento Gosho:
a timber and turf bridge.**
The soft qualities of wood associate well with the organic forms of rocks and plants. The bed of the stream is given interest by scattering it with flat stones like those on the beach.

65

Two Gardens of the Italian Renaissance

Villa d'Este, Tivoli: 1550   Architect: Pirro Ligorio

Villa Lante, Bagnaio: c. 1566   Architect: Vignola

At the very time when the Mughuls were beginning their quest for an earthly paradise a new kind of garden was evolving in Italy. Based on the classical Roman garden with its geometry and sculptural green forms, the new gardens were an expression of Renaissance man's attitude to nature: man was the centre of the universe and need no longer fear nature. The garden then became a projection of the house into the landscape, relying for its beauty on the reconciliation of man's ordered mind with organic natural forms.

More Roman in spirit than almost all other Italian Renaissance gardens, with monumental terraces set on a steep hillside, the Villa d'Este well expresses the pomp and circumstance of the Papacy in the sixteenth century. It is only twenty miles from Rome and was built for Cardinal Ippolito d'Este, for whose entertainments it provided a spectacular setting.

The situation is dramatic, with a glorious view and a river at the highest point, whence it was diverted through the garden. At each level the water takes on a different shape and a fresh intonation, the architecture echoing the music of the water in its variety. The overall plan is geometric, with perspectives looking down across the terraces at right-angles and with straight ramps leading from one terrace to the next.

Like the Mughul gardens, the Villa itself was to be approached from below, through a *bosco* or grove, past huge fish-ponds with a fountain complex known as the organ at one end, towards terraces of increasing magnificence and dazzling abundance of fountains. Finally the top terrace is reached and with it the sweeping view over the Roman *campagna*.

The terrace of the 100 fountains, with Este eagles and other stone emblems.

The oval pool.

The water staircase, with water channels in the top of the outer balustrades.

The organ.

With Lante the Italian Renaissance garden reached perfection. The simple harmony of its plan and the inventive use of water set it above all other gardens of the period, lovely though they were. Nature, here docile and gentle, is the dominating genius of the place and man's willing submission is symbolised by the division of the house into two pavilions, one on each side of the central axis. For although the patron for whom Lante was built was also a prince of the Church, Cardinal Gambara was a lover of nature as well as a cultivated churchman.

The whole design of the garden is etched in water. From the rock face at the top (the garden is set on a hillside near Viterbo) a little waterfall fills a rough stone pool. The water is then led down the centre of the garden in stages each more sophisticated than the last until it reaches the water-parterre at the bottom. The entrance to the garden is at this level and is reached by steps which pass above a large curved pool with sculpture by Giambologna in the centre. This pool has a crucial function since it links the formal garden with its counter-balance, the half-wild woodland threaded with paths and occasional fountain jets.

The curved pool with Giambologna's equestrian statue. On the right a path vanishes into the woodlands.

The water-parterre and one of the two pavilions.

The water-parterre from above.

A fountain on the main axis.

The "fountain of the little lights".

Between the two fountains was a dining terrace with a stone table. Water runs down the middle of the table, to cool the wine or perhaps to float little dishes as in Pliny's day.

A rill enclosed by stone fish. In later gardens the rill became a cascade, as at Collodi.

ITALY

Isola Bella, Lake Maggiore

c. 1630–1670   Architects: Angelo Crivelli and Carlo Fontana

The marble ships which so delighted the Chinese Emperors are outclassed by this splendid Borromean galleon, with its ten terraces rising above the water like the stern of a ship and its silhouette of masts and spars.

Its originator, Count Carlo Borromeo, searching perhaps for a paradise among the Italian lakes and therefore looking beyond the confines of his own domain, gave distinction to Isola Bella by treating the whole environment as one design. This overriding idea, and the simple land-forms made by levelling the island, closely relate the garden to the water and counterbalance the baroque theatricality of the details.

The island is two-thirds garden, one-third palace.

(above)
Magnolias, camellias, pomegranates and citrus trees soften the lines of the terraces while jasmine and roses fill the air with their scent.

(below)
A piece of pure stage scenery, the product of a theatrical age.

Château de Chantilly, near Paris

1622   Architect: Le Nôtre

Versailles may be Le Nôtre's most famous garden and Vaux-le-Vicomte the most accomplished, but Chantilly is unquestionably his greatest water garden. Here he used his mastery of space design to evolve from not very promising conditions a composition equal in splendour to that of his patron, Le Grand Condé.

The chateau itself was built on a small rock in the midst of ponds and marshes. As a mass, it was too small to serve as a focal point of a vast new landscape in harmony with the times. Le Nôtre's genius lay in swinging the main axis of the new design to one side of the chateau, thereby leaving himself free to plan a lay-out on a much larger scale than would otherwise have been possible.

Unlike Versailles, there was plenty of water at Chantilly and Le Nôtre made the most of it. From the moated chateau the Duke could look down on the great water-parterre, sparkling with fountains on great occasions or at other times still as mirrors reflecting the sky. Some of the pools are in fact shaped like the mirrors of the period. Beyond the water-parterre was a braod cross canal, as at Vaux. A massive flight of steps, themselves flowing downward like water, leads from the water-parterre to the formal approach drive which continues the axis across the road as a forest ride. On the opposite side of the chateau there was a flower-parterre with high-leaping fountains but this has been replaced by an "English garden".

The gardens were primarily a setting for entertainment. Saint-Simon, in his memoirs, describes one such *fête* given for the Duchesse de Berry, when "lavishness, gaiety and magnificence, fantasies and delightful surprises continued unceasingly". The *fête* nearly ended in tragedy, however, for a tiger escaped from the menagerie which the Duke kept on the further side of the canal. It caused panic among the musicians, actors and actresses who were to entertain the guests, but was recaptured before it could do any harm.*

* From *The Historical Memoirs of the Duc de Saint-Simon*, edited and translated by Lucy Norton, vol. III (Hamish Hamilton).

An aerial view shows the lay-out. The cross canal joins on to the end of the large water-basin in the centre foreground.

The water-parterre today, with the cross canal cutting through the middle of the picture.

A bird's eye view, from a drawing by Perelle.

(below)
The grand cascade, from a drawing by Perelle.

ITALY

Villa Garzoni, Collodi

c. 1652

In the history of water architecture the garden of the Villa Garzoni is interesting for its treatment of the central water feature, poised in time between Lante (1566) with its gentle rill and the tremendous, never-ending cascades of Caserta (1752) which abruptly turn into a canal in the French manner.

In two earlier gardens, the Villas Aldobrandini and Torlonia at Frascati, the central rill had broadened into a cascade. Garzoni followed later and here, through groves of ilex, the water tumbles down over rocks that outline a giant's face, with stone staircases on either side.

The plan (of great beauty even to those who normally dislike the baroque) was dictated by the site. The original castle was perched above the valley in such a position that it was only possible to make a garden to one side. Hence the domestic part of the garden – the enchanting bath-house, the open-air theatre and the shady walks – are in the upper part of the garden. The formal parterre is at the foot of the classical Roman terraces which extend across the foot of the cascade.

The central axis. The cascade is above the formal terraces.

Looking down the water staircase towards the bottom parterre where fountains in the two circular pools throw their jets forty feet into the air.

The grotto at the foot of the water staircase. At this point the water disappears under the terraces.

The hedge with its strong rhythms separates the garden from the Villa, from whose window the parterres can be seen spread out like a carpet.

Chatsworth, Derbyshire

c. 1688–1707; c. 1755–1764; 1800–1858

The English climate has never called for the large-scale use of water in swift motion, whether leaping or cascading, nor do the land-forms lend themselves to such devices. Chatsworth is almost unique in this country in having water at a high level to provide power for cascades and fountains and the three Dukes of Devonshire who contributed to the garden's lay-out made the most of their opportunities.

At the time when the first Duke began the rebuilding of the house and the creation of a new garden, England was absorbing the Renaissance. It is therefore not surprising that the influence of France and Italy made itself felt at Chatsworth. The Great Cascade was planned by a Frenchman named Grillet and finished in 1696, only to be uprooted five years later and rebuilt on a larger scale, with a wider, steeper and longer flight and a pavilion at its head, designed by Thomas Archer. The uprooting was probably to help dispose of unwanted soil from a hillock which the Duke had had levelled so that he could see the surrounding landscape.

The sea-horse fountain on the south front dates from this period, although then it was surrounded by a parterre garden. The original willow tree fountain, ancestor of the present copper tree, was made in 1693 and stood with its jets playing from the tips of its branches in the centre of a large square plantation, according to a perspective drawing by Kniff. There were numerous other fountains, all supplied from lakes dug out at the top of the hill.

So much formality was not to the taste of the fourth Duke, who inherited Chatsworth just as the English Landscape School was sweeping all before it. Here as elsewhere terraces were demolished, parterres vanished and the gardens took on their present park-like aspect under the guidance of Capability Brown.

The sixth Duke brought back some degree of formality. He was responsible for the immensely high fountain in the canal on the south front, known as the Emperor's fountain because it was the Duke's riposte to the fountains of Peterhof, which he had seen at the coronation of Czar Nicholas I of Russia in 1826. That same year Joseph Paxton was appointed head gardener at Chatsworth, an event that was to lead to many and varied developments, such as the great conservatory, precursor of the Crystal Palace, and the aqueduct cascade, an imposing but slightly clumsy Victorian conceit.

The Great Cascade with Archer's pavilion at the top.

(left)
The sea-horse fountain. The sculpture is by Cibber.

(below)
The Emperor's fountain.

The copper tree, a reproduction made in 1829 of
the original willow tree fountain of 1693.

Paxton's aqueduct cascade.

87

Westbury Court, Gloucestershire

c. 1697–1705

Echoes of the flat landscape of Holland float about the canals of Westbury, begun some ten years after the accession of William III. Dutch influence then began to make itself felt in the arts: in garden design its chief effect was to bring home the suitability of tranquil water in our geographic and climatic conditions.

Westbury is virtually the only Dutch water garden to survive in England. Set in flat country near the river Severn, it is a total water landscape which accepts the implications of its situation. The main features are two canals, one running from a *clairvoyée* on the road straight towards a small pavilion, the other parallel but T-shaped at one end.

In the early 1960's the garden was allowed to fall into decay but it is now being restored by Gloucestershire County Council.

An engraving of the house and gardens by Kip, published in 1712. The horizontal lines of the canals are relieved by the verticality of the buildings, particularly the church spire and the pavilion, which was originally supported on six Ionic pillars. These were bricked in about 1895. The second canal can be seen on the further side of that which terminates in the pavilion.

88

(above)
The long canal in 1908. Hedges played an important part in Dutch gardens, giving a sense of enclosure from the surrounding flat countryside. Records show that 1,000 yews were supplied in 1699 to Maynard Colchester, for whom Westbury was built.

(below)
Looking across the T-canal towards the pavilion: a photograph taken in 1908. The Victorian house was pulled down in 1961.

Casa dos Marques de Fronteira, Bemfica

c. 1700

Moorish traditions and the inspiration of the Italian Renaissance form the basis of Portuguese garden design, with an added touch of richness and fantasy – trace-elements of Portugal's colonial and sea-faring history.

All these influences are at work at Fronteira: the Italianate parterre with its axial planning and geometric box hedges; the Moorish water-tank and use of tiles, particularly in the little gallery above the water-tank; and the exuberant stonework of the little enclosed fountain. But in each case the influences have been assimilated and digested, reappearing in a style which is essentially Portuguese.

Fronteira was begun at the end of the seventeenth century and finished in 1712, a period when Portugal was successfully reasserting herself as a great power both in Europe and in South America. This moment of expansion is reflected in the air of serene confidence which pervades the garden and in the mastery of materials.

The parterre: the garden is some fifteen feet lower than the house and is surrounded by walls, balustrades and parapets.

(above)
Above the water-tank are blue and white tiles portraying the twelve Portuguese knights who, according to legend, went to England to defend the honour of twelve English ladies and returned victorious.

(left)
The enclosed fountain:
The strong swirling lines of the stone-work recall the movement of Portugal's Atlantic rollers.

91

The Zwinger, Dresden

c. 1714   Architect: Daniel Pöppelmann

Walter Pater wrote that all art constantly aspires towards the condition of music. Of the Zwinger it might be said that its architecture aspires towards the condition of water, for the union of architecture with fountain forms is complete. The pavilions resemble huge clusters of tall, foaming jets such as appear in the Rigaud and Perelle prints of Versailles, while the rhythmic series of rounded windows recall the fine interlocking sprays of Moorish origin. The whole of the detail, too, has water movement.

The Zwinger was originally the orangery for a vast palace, planned but never completed, for Augustus the Strong of Saxony. It was inspired by Versailles, like many other German gardens of the day, each of the princely owners interpreting Le Nôtre's ideas in his own slightly individualistic manner.

The lay-out is conventional. Within the rectangular site, corridors enclose the central garden court in a square with large apses on two opposite sides, round which were grouped buildings for different forms of entertainment. In the centre of the garden court are four curving fountain pools. Originally, these were surrounded by elaborate *broderies* which linked garden and buildings more effectively than the plain grass plots which took their place, and gave the whole composition the character of a garden palace.

The Zwinger was destroyed by Allied bombing in February 1945 but has since been splendidly restored.

(above)
The central garden court with one of the two apses.

(below left)
Water-associated sculpture along the inner wall of one of the two side corridors.

(below right)
The Nymphenbad

Peterhof (Petrodvorets) near Leningrad

c. 1715 Architect: Le Blond

Peterhof, a dazzling *tour de force* built by Peter the Great, stands on a bluff overlooking the Gulf of Finland near Leningrad. It was intended as a rival to Versailles and was designed by a Frenchman but, as so often happened in Russian art and architecture, the ideas which inspired it seem to have passed through the Russian digestive process, emerging with a distinctive national aura. At Peterhof this finds expression in the rich use of coloured marble, the profusion and exuberance of the fountains and the gold of the statues.

The lay-out in front of the palace is formal and architectural, with a double water staircase of coloured marble flanking a large basin. From this, water falls over more steps into a broad straight canal cutting between thickly planted trees to link the palace with the sea in one grand waterscape.

The grand cascade.
The garden has been magnificently restored since the war.

(above)
A gold statue of Samson struggling with the lion, which stands at the foot of the cascade. The jet from the lion's mouth leaps high into the air.

(left)
The canal to the sea.
The entire area between the sea and the terrace was laid out as a park with fountains at the crossing-points of the avenues. It was a major operation, calling for whole ship-loads of trees and plants.

95

Stourhead, Wiltshire

1714–1764

Unlike the waters of Katsura, the lake landscape of Stourhead is concerned less with nature than with man's interpretation of it. This is no evocation of wild scenery but an idyllic landscape with classical overtones, seen through a painter's eye.

The lake is the focal point of the garden's philosophy and design. It is the foreground for the Claude-like compositions of tree-girt temples on grassy knolls that shimmer across its calm unbroken expanse. "Incidents" such as these are linked by a path round the lake that leads from the Temple of Flora, through grottoes presided over by the Nymph of the Grot and the River God, to the Pantheon, finally climbing to the Temple of the Sun set high above the lake. Behind this journey lies a deep philosophical meaning: it symbolises man's progress through life. Henry Hoare, owner and creator of the garden, shared his contemporaries' feeling of kinship with classical Rome and there is evidence that, in planning Stourhead, he had in mind Virgil's account of the wanderings of Aeneas and his descent into the underworld at Lake Avernus.

The idea of a circular garden walk leading from one point of interest to another was still in its infancy at this time, while Pope's advice to "Consult the genius of the place . . . that . . . paints as you plant and as you work, designs" had not yet resulted in more than a scattering of consciously picturesque landscapes. But Hoare's greatest stroke was perhaps the wooded lake. Created from barren downland and a few fish-ponds, it was one of the first of the artificial lakes which were such a characteristic feature of all subsequent English landscape design.

The Pantheon, designed by Flitcroft, seen across the lake from the entrance to the garden.
The composition is closely modelled on Claude Lorrain's "Coast View of Delos with Aeneas". The
smaller building on the right is the Rustic Cottage, a slightly later addition.

The grotto of the River God, second of the two grottoes, which are approached by a tunnel of rough tufa and flint, lit by shafts of light, suggesting the descent into the underworld. The waters of the Stour pour from the god's overturned urn, spreading across the floor of the grotto.

The craggy arch across the path up from the lake to the Temple of the Sun suggests the gateway to Lake Avernus.

Fontana di Trevi, Rome

1762   Architect: Nicola Salvi

The water supply of modern Rome is based on the system constructed by the ancient Romans in the first and second centuries A.D. In 52 A.D. eight aqueducts brought water to the capital from the surrounding hills, sometimes over long distances, each delivering the water direct to its own *castellum* or display fountain. There were no reservoirs and no mingling of water from different sources. The network developed over the years and by the first Gothic sack of Rome in 410 A.D. eleven aqueducts were feeding 1,212 public fountains, 11 imperial baths and 926 public baths. It has been continuously maintained and developed.

The Fontana di Trevi is fed by the Acqua Vergine Nova which has its source about nine miles east of Rome, towards Tivoli. The first Trevi fountain was a plain wall fountain designed by Leone Battista Alberti in the 1450's. In 1640 Pope Urban VIII asked Giovanni Bernini to design a new fountain, but Bernini died before his plans were complete, although he had pulled down the old fountain and re-sited it in its present position so that it could be seen by the Pope from his summer residence on the Quirinal. Delay followed delay and it was only after 122 years and several Popes had vanished into the mists of time that the fountain was rebuilt, to a design by Nicola Salvi.

The fountain is a remarkable fusion of architecture and rock forms: these last are not so much naturalistic as abstract. The inspiration may have come from the chasm at Tivoli but the forms themselves were such as to appeal to the baroque taste of the period.

Veduta in prospettiva della gran Fontana dell'Acqua Vergine detta di Trevi. Architettura di Nicola Salvi.

An engraving by Piranesi.

The water is ingeniously distributed in its several channels.

The statues are the key to the composition. Man is the centre of the world that comprehends and unites civilised architecture and wild rocks.

Palazzo Reale, Caserta

1752   Architect: Luigi Vanvitelli

For sheer opulence and exuberance, this must surely be the most stupendous single water project ever executed.

The park was laid out for Charles III, a grandson of Louis XIV and son of King Philip V of Spain, and the influence of France and Spain is discernible in the design. Charles III had spent part of his childhood at La Granja, not far from Madrid, the garden of which was itself modelled on Versailles. As Georgina Masson has pointed out in her book *Italian Gardens*, the line of development which had passed from Italy to France and thence to Spain had now come full circle.

The enormously broad central vista is some two miles in length. In the centre, a cascade tumbling down from low hills becomes a water staircase far wider and more sophisticated than that at Collodi, and this in turn becomes a French canal, interrupted at intervals by changes of level each marked by a fountain.

This was the last explosion of Italian baroque but decadent though it may be when set beside, for example, the Trevi fountain, one has only to compare it with the slightly earlier Peterhof to appreciate the superiority of Italian design.

The cascade, the culmination of the traditional Italian design.

The Fountain of Diana:
From here begins the long sweep down to the palace.

The water staircase:
The vista is contained within a double line of clipped trees behind
which are formal wooded areas.

The Backs, Cambridge

c. 1755–1775

That this idyllic landscape was once a scene of busy commerce is hard to imagine, but so it was. When Henry VI founded King's College in 1441 the land he bought was partly covered with tenements and other buildings, and along the river Cam between Queen's College and Magdalene College were wharves and hythes where barges loaded and unloaded. These earlier buildings were eventually pulled down but even then the river played no part in the life of the university, most of the colleges being cut off from it by walls. Wren's library for Trinity College, begun in 1676, turns a relatively austere face to the river compared with the facade towards the college.

It was not until 1725 that the first winds of romanticism came wafting uncertainly across the fens to Cambridge. In that year Charles Bridgeman, a pioneer of the English School of Landscape Gardening, was called in by King's College to advise on the lay-out of the ground between the river and the college buildings, but nothing seems to have come of this and it was not until 1775–6 that the wall along the river was lowered, probably at the suggestion of James Essex junior.

Meanwhile, the ideas generated by the early romantic gardens such as Stourhead were spreading to a wider audience and some of the Cambridge colleges had begun to open up their river frontages. The Fellows of St. John's College had their garden laid out in 1752 by no less a person than Capability Brown. Brown, unasked, also did a plan which treated the whole river area between Peterhouse and Magdalene as one design, with King's College occupying the position usually taken by the mansion in Brown's designs and St. John's College relegated to the humbler role of the stables.

Although this design was never carried out, it is almost as if it had been, for today the colleges are all linked in one philosophical landscape which is an integral part of the university's way of life. Here the mind finds release in the contrast between the enclosed college courts, which are finite, and the river, which is infinite.

King's College chapel (On the left is Clare College).

Trinity bridge and the avenue across the meadows.

St. John's College:
The stone bridge has replaced the earlier agricultural wooden structure.

ENGLAND

The Thames, London

Eighteenth Century

"With that I saw two Swans of goodly hue,
Come softly swimming down along the Lee . . .
So purely white they were,
That even the gentle stream, the which them bare,
Seem'd foul to them, and bade his billows spare
To wet their silken feathers, lest they might
Soil their fair plumes with water not so fair . . .
Sweet Thames, run softly, till I end my Song."

These lines from Edmund Spenser's *Prothalamion* were written towards the end of the sixteenth century. Even then pollution of the river had begun, but its beauty was at its height. The river retained its charm and increased its grandeur for the next two centuries: Addison described it in *The Spectator* as "the noblest river in Europe". Today there is a desire to restore it to its former glory, and of all the records of its history in illustration, poetry and music, none are so compelling and inspiring as those of the eighteenth century.

The river rises in the Cotswolds and passes by towns and villages and agricultural scenery, gradually growing in stature as it skirts Windsor and approaches London. Everything indicates that in the eighteenth century it was busy with commerce and pleasure. The buildings beside it were so designed and placed that individually they enriched the scene. At Twickenham, with Alexander Pope's villa, the landscape was still rural and domestic. The river then widens, becoming tidal; unlike those of the narrower Seine in Paris, each bank of the Thames becomes a backcloth disassociated from the opposite side.

The north bank was the more imposing, for here lay the Cities of Westminster and London. The Abbey and St. Paul's marked the two domains: between them and facing south over the river stretched the great establishments and gardens of the nobility and wealthy merchants. The curves unfolded a panorama whose silhouette was broken by countless church spires that seemed to echo the masts of the ships. The river scene was impressively closed by London Bridge. Onwards, perilously under the bridge, past the Tower of London, the busy docks and warehouses, and so to Greenwich Palace, a fitting climax before the river finally broadens into estuary and sea.

By the end of the nineteenth century the decline of the river was recognised by all and lamented by William Morris in his prologue to *The Wanderers*:

"Forget six counties overhung with smoke,
Forget the snorting steam and piston stroke,
Forget the spreading of the hideous town;
Think rather of the pack-horse on the down,
And dream of London, small and white and clean,
The clear Thames bordered by its gardens green."

The only great river sceneries today left to London that fully convey the previous grandeur are those of Greenwich Palace, the Houses of Parliament at Westminster and the Tower with Tower Bridge. Hampton Court and Chelsea Hospital are detached. Somerset House has been severed from the water by the embankment road. St. Thomas's Hospital, with its sequence of buildings suggesting an affinity with the ebb and flow of the tide, has been pulled down to make way for a building that might be anywhere. The South Bank complex has been a valiant attempt to restore the river to its rightful place and the views from the terrace might well have been without equal were it not that they are stifled by Charing Cross railway bridge. At low tide the river is sordid. The time must come when a barrage will keep the water at a constant level, creating site values much greater than at present, and cause the river to become once again London's most spectacular park and "the noblest river in Europe".

(above)
The Thames at Twickenham:
Fashionable villas in varying styles of architecture — Chinese, Gothic revival and classical — lined the river bank. Alexander Pope's villa is to the left of the domed building. From a drawing by H. Muntz.

(below)
The City from Somerset Gardens:
From a painting by Canaletto. London Bridge can be seen in the distance. The river at this time was a great thoroughfare for traffic of all kinds.

Greenwich Palace: Nelson's funeral, drawn by Pugin. Designed mainly by Sir Christopher Wren,
the complex is the finest early eighteenth century land and waterscape left in England.

Brighton, Sussex

1800–1900

Brighton came into full flower as a fashionable resort in the 1780's, just as the English romantic movement was beginning to lose its purity and turn to exoticism. In the search for the strange and the fantastic, romantic ideas were culled from all over the world, especially from the East, and nowhere were they put into practice more eagerly than in Brighton at the turn of the century. Or more appropriately, for the seaside has long been considered an excuse for putting on fancy dress.

The earliest of the Brighton fantasies was the Prince Regent's Royal Pavilion. First planned as an Indian palace in 1805 but not completed until about 1821, its domes would not have looked out of place in Coleridge's *Xanadu*, written a few years earlier. Next came the Chain Pier, with a strong Egyptian flavour, built in 1823 to serve passenger traffic between England and France. Later the West Pier (1866) and Palace Pier (1891) reverted to the Indian style, with golden Mughul turrets as well as domes. Meanwhile, the terraces of houses built along the front continued the tradition of ordered classicism.

In their different ways each of these buildings has a specific relationship to the sea. The fragility of the piers and the frivolity of the pavilion emphasize its enduring vastness; the long terraces are the landward counterpart of the lines of the waves on the foreshore.

The Chain Pier and the Pavilion:
An engraving from a painting by J. M. W. Turner. The Chain Pier was destroyed in a storm in 1896.

The Royal Pavilion, designed by John Nash.

116

Palace Pier.

(below)
Sea images are worked into the design of the seats on West Pier. The pattern of the back-support is like the lacey fret of a retreating wave: the divisions between the seats are based on the lamprey.

Ashford Castle, Cong

1852–1915

Ashford Castle is a product of the English romantic movement, which reached its climax in the mid-nineteenth century, and of the affluence of the industrial age. It is an attempt to escape from that age into a world of romance enclosed in a landscape of great beauty: an attempt on the heroic scale which must have failed without the wealth provided by that same industrialism which it sought to forget.

The castle stands at the head of Lough Corrib, a rugged cliff of a building in the baronial style beloved of the Victorians, superimposed upon an eighteenth century shooting lodge and the remains of a medieval tower. Its massive forms, softened by their pseudo-romanticism, give a sense of cohesion to the gentle Irish scene that spreads about them. From the battlements the landscape appears poised between heaven and earth.

The development of the Ashford estate was begun by Sir Benjamin Lee Guinness and continued by his son, Lord Ardilaun, who conceived and executed the design. Today the castle is a hotel, thus continuing to provide escapism in time and space.

The River Cong joins Lough Corrib beside the castle. In the classical garden the round pool is beautifully set in relation to the curve of the river.

(above)
So immersed was Lord Ardilaun by his love for the lake landscape that he directed his body to be buried on the island from which he took his name.

(below)
Bent on getting the best of all worlds, only the Victorians would have thought of combining a classical garden with medieval architecture, but the result is surprisingly harmonious.

Schlossgarten, Stuttgart

1961

Once the garden of a palace, the Schlossgarten today provides a green setting for the town's relaxation. It lies at the very centre of the town yet despite its two-mile length it is so contrived that there is no contact with traffic other than by a passing glance from the elegant bridge linking one part with another.

At one end a concert hall, an art gallery and a theatre are grouped round a large lake, a survival from the earlier garden. This double theme of entertainment and water carries over into the rest of the garden, mainly through the lavish use of fountains that have an element of fun as well as charm – true water games, to give a literal translation of their German name, "Wasserspiele". Their variety is seemingly endless, for the Germans are adepts at exploiting the potentialities of water and might almost be said to have evolved a new art form.

The gaiety and inventiveness of the water forms are not only amusing to watch: they are an invitation to explore deeper into the garden in search of fresh diversions. It is the same planning principle as at Stourhead but the role of the temples is here played by fountains.

The cascade fountain, designed by Peter Faller.

In a setting of bubble fountains a river god reclines among hostas, iris and other water-associated plants.

(above)
Details such as pools, stepping stones and cascades are designed and executed with complete mastery of technique and are impeccably maintained.

(below)
The grass-like leaves of *Iris sibirica* echo the fine spray of the fountain jets. Throughout the garden the planting is related to the water forms.

International Garden Exhibition, Hamburg

1963

Exhibition gardens are by their very nature more highly keyed than other types of garden. They must vibrate with movement and a sense of things happening. The Hamburg designers relied largely on water to create this atmosphere, using it in many ingeniously contrived forms, including a demonstration that water *can* be made to go up hill.

There is an excellent system in Germany whereby, every two or three years, the larger towns take their turn to stage a national garden exhibition. The design of the lay-out is usually decided by a competition, the winning scheme being carried out by the town authorities. For two years the public are charged an entrance fee which is offset against the construction costs, after which the garden becomes the town park. By this means the town acquires a park which is much more lavish than it could normally afford, and at a lower cost.

The most spectacular of the water features, on a scale large enough to be enjoyed from the overhead cable railway. Watching it is rather like watching the sea – the water never repeats its effects.

Even the flat water scenes are given a sense of movement by the lines of stepping stones.

A water feature enlivening the otherwise dead area of a pedestrian underpass. It is illuminated at night.

Mexico City

Museum of Anthropology (1964)
New Chapultepec Park

Mexico City stands on the site of the old Aztec capital of Tenochtitlan which, before its destruction by the Spaniards in 1521, must have been one of the most beautiful waterscapes ever known. The city was built on islands in the western part of Lake Tezcuco. Canals threaded through every part; causeways linked the islands with the lake shore; while the waters outside the city were dotted with man-made floating islands. "Fairy islands of flowers" Prescott calls them, "overshadowed occasionally by trees of considerable size, rising and falling with the gentle undulation of the billows". He also says that the courts of Montezuma's palace were cooled by fountains fed by a reservoir on the distant hill of Chapultepec, which supplied enough water for more than a hundred palace baths.

Today the lake has shrunk and is some three miles from Mexico City. The tradition of water survives, however, and has recently burst forth in some remarkable water designs. In these, traditional archaic forms have been translated into a modern idiom and combined with present-day techniques. Robust in character and tumultuous in sound, their profusion challenges the Villa d'Este at Tivoli, perhaps the only European garden where water in motion is used with such abundance.

Museum of Anthropology.
An aluminium canopy is suspended over a courtyard of the museum by means of stays from the top of a central sculptured column, rather like an inverted half-open umbrella. From the canopy falls a vertical curtain of water, which then disappears through holes in the ground and is pumped back to the top again through the central column. The movement and sound of the water bring the museum to life.

New Chapultepec Park, on the outskirts of Mexico City.
In a huge pool some 50 feet across, a water-god lies on his back with arms outstretched. His head, seen here, resembles the mask of a jaguar, patterned in coloured stone-work.

New Chapultepec Park.

(above)
The sculptured heads are a modern interpretation of Aztec forms. Behind them, water curtains fall from the parapets of white walls that are decorated with stylised motifs of insects and animals.

(below)
From the outer wall of the park spring innumerable jets, very like the terrace of 100 fountains at the Villa d'Este, Tivoli.

The University, York

1964–1968   Architects: Robert Matthew, Johnson-Marshall & Partners

Necessity and invention have joined hands to good effect in the landscape design for York University. It was the need for a balancing reservoir for the land drainage and surface water system that led to the creation of the artificial lake which is the core of the whole scheme, uniting the buildings round one central idea. The opportunities for pleasure and drama thus offered have been whole-heartedly taken up by the architects. Water has been introduced into the courts of some of the buildings, while students cross from one part of the university to another on a series of light foot-bridges. Terraces overlook the lake and a small garden of bog and marginal plants has been established. One is again reminded of the lake at Stourhead surrounded by its classical buildings.

In much the same way as the Greeks used light reflected from white marble paving to illuminate the friezes of the Parthenon, so at York the light reflected off the lake gives a flickering luminosity to the buildings grouped round its verges.

Aerial view. The lake is lined with polythene covered with gravel and soil.

132

Central Hall: the overhanging forms rising from the water, like terraces upside down, are reminiscent of Isola Bella.

(above)
The terrace of Vanbrugh College. The water steps are perhaps the most essential feature of the design.

(below)
A covered way crosses the weir connecting the water courtyard of Derwent College with the head of the lake.

Lovejoy Plaza, Portland, Oregan

1966   Landscape Architects: Larence Halprin & Associates

Audience participation at the Trevi fountain in Rome is generally confined to the throwing of coins. Lovejoy Plaza was deliberately designed for maximum participation and there are no limits. People of all ages clamber up the wet rocks; they plunge through a wall of water; they even, it seems, marry in it.

Though so unlike in this respect, their abstract rock forms seem to link the two across the centuries, yet here again there are basic differences. In Rome, the emphasis is on the rocks and figures, which are probably inspired by Tivoli with its classical associations: the importance of man in the natural order is manifest. In Portland, the inspiration came from the wild mountain waterfalls of the High Sierras, here re-created in essence; the interest and complexity centre on the water. The rocks are there to break up the flow, so that people may experience contact with the spray and allow themselves to be engulfed in the thunder and foam of the torrent.

An aerial view.

135

Sea City

2000   Architect: Hal Moggridge with John Martin and Ken Anthony

This is a theoretical exercise, initiated by the Pilkington Glass Age Committee in 1968, to explore one possible solution to the problem of overcrowding in Britain.

For an island nation with a seafaring history there is a strong appeal in the idea of building a city in off-shore shoal waters. Sea City would stand on concrete stilts and would be protected by a floating breakwater and a curved 180 foot high wall. It would be a self-contained community of 30,000 inhabitants.

Its functional shape, dictated by geographical and climatic conditions, takes us back to the shells of the opening chapter.

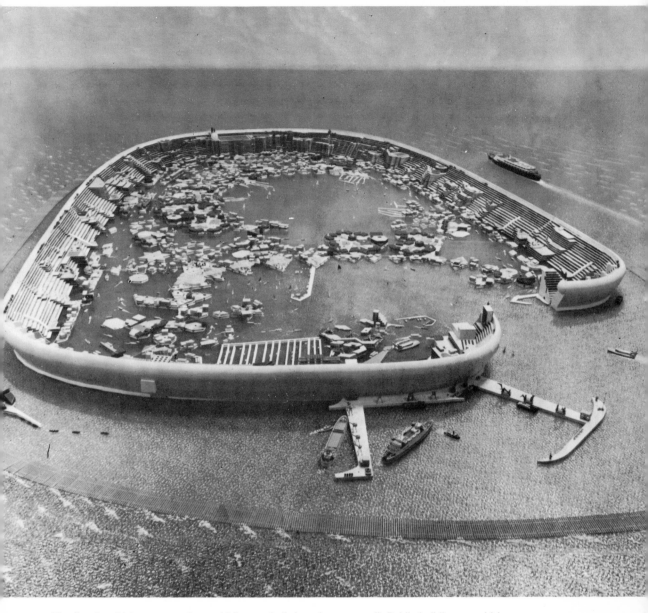

The flats in which most people would live are built into the outer wall. Public buildings would be on the floating islands in the central lagoon.